CHASING
PORCUPINES

How to Lead Prickly People

STEVEN IWERSEN

Aurora Pointe LLC

Aurora Pointe, LLC
15621 W 87th St. #144
Lenexa, KS 66219

ISBN-13: 978-0-9824045-0-8
ISBN-10: 0-9824045-0-6

PRINTED IN THE UNITED STATES OF AMERICA

Ordering Information:
Special discounts are available on quantity purchases by corporations, associations, and others for sales promotions or premiums. Special editions, including personalized covers, excerpts of existing books and corporate imprints, can be created in large quantities for special needs. For details, contact Aurora Pointe, LLC by writing to the above address or phone 913-406-3824.

To my parents
Rev. GW and Sherry Iwersen

Who modeled selfless leadership
and gave me the gift of love, respect and
permission to explore the possibilities.

To my grandfather
Willard E. Palmer, ENCM

Who served his country faithfully for
43 years active duty in the US Navy,
and taught me the most profound
leadership lessons by living out his convictions
and loving his wife and family exceptionally.

CHASING
PORCUPINES

CONTENTS

FORWARD

The world is filled with speakers, trainers, and consultants who have good ideas, excellent strategies, and sound counsel. And every now and then you run across a special person who gives you more. Steven Iwersen is that very special person.

Steven has excellent strategies, tips, and practical ideas for helping you deal with prickly people, as you're about to discover in this book. He also has a boundless amount of wisdom that comes from having put these strategies and suggestions into practice himself. He is a living role model of commitment, integrity, and leadership excellence.

A former pastor, Steven is deeply committed to leading, living, and interacting with a distinct set of values. And, when you have a sense of clarity that comes from knowing who you are and what you stand for, then your wisdom, insights, and strategies take on a whole new depth of meaning. That's what I like about this book.

If you ever have a chance to hear Steven speak, take advantage of that opportunity. And, if you have a chance to hear him sing, you'll find out he's a remarkable jazz vocalist. By the same token, if you ever have a chance to meet him personally, you will be one of the lucky ones. Whenever I spend time with Steven, I walk away a better person.

Read every word in this book and put Steven's suggestions into practice. You'll be glad you did and the lasting impact can be profound. It certainly has been for me.

~ Chuc Barnes , CSP
MinutesCount!
Author of "Get Your Ducks in A Row"
and "Capture the Moment"

ACKNOWLEDGMENTS

When asked what I wanted to be when I grew up, I'd say: "a writer, one that lives in a cabin by a mountain lake, with a typewriter, a cup of coffee, and a morning fog lifting from the water." That was inspiration! I'd like to express my appreciation to all the people who dared to ask me what I wanted to be.

Thank you to Jackie Neely, my 7th Grade English teacher, for teaching me more about writing than I ever learned in college. Thank you to Mrs. Anderson, who inspired a future professional speaker during Senior speech class.

Thanks to all those for whom I've had the honor of serving as a leader.

Thanks to my dearest friends in the National Speakers Association for welcoming me into the family. Thank you to my Mastermind partners, Chuc Barnes, Cathy Newton and Candy Whirley for your creativity and the accountability.

To my sons: Daniel, Ben and Andrew, I cherish our memories of laughing, wrestling, telling silly stories and fishing. I cherish more the friendship we have today.

Brandy, you are my best friend and greatest source of encouragement. Thank you so much for being my wife. You *Fly Me To The Moon*!

Finally, thanks to God for His *mercies are new every morning*! I have been a grateful recipient.

INTRODUCTION

I can only imagine the variety of reasons that may have prompted you to pick up this book. You:

- Thought this was a book about porcupines and how you could keep them from consuming your garden,
- Smiled at the title and thought it was interesting,
- Could relate to the title and have some "Prickly People" in your life that you'd like to chase off,
- Want to find a simple approach with practical ideas that could help you deal with those "prickly" issues of leading people through change, conflict management, and keeping a good attitude in spite of it all!

I won't be able to help you with the garden problems. This is not a book about the study of the *Erethizon dorsatum* species of rodents. This is a book about the wonders of leading the human species when they bristle and become defensive. It also points out some practical insights on what to do when we, as leaders, are feeling prickly.

If you're looking for a comprehensive book that addresses conflict with an empirical study and presents the 27 steps that you must know and take in absolute perfect sequence in order to be the ideal leader, this is not the book for you. But if you are looking for a quick read that states the obvious, encourages the practical, gives simple strategies and inspires you to be a better leader; this may be the very thing you were looking for.

WHAT PEOPLE WANT

The reality of leadership becomes quite apparent within a short period of time for most new leaders: we are hired to be leaders, but what most people want is a "hired hand."

- Leaders focus attention on what *needs* to be done.
- People expect leaders to do what they *want* done.

- Leaders are expected to accomplish results *with* people.
- The people we lead expect to accomplish the results *without* having to change.

- Leaders want to succeed.
- Some people want to see us fail.

Now don't panic; the reality of leadership also entails the truth that most people want to see you succeed! Very few people want their leader to be a failure. That would be like going to a concert and hoping that the singer can't carry a tune or stay on the melody! No one wants that kind of torture. The majority of us hope that our leaders will be able to step into the spotlight and be able to do more than just mediocre karaoke – we want professional quality that includes an encore!

So be encouraged, you have a cheering fan club! You have people who are looking for you to provide a sense of direction amidst the chaos. They want someone to sort through the everyday details and inspire them to something bigger, something significant. They will defend you and give every effort to be on your winning team. And they need you (they want you) to know how to deal with the negative people that often sabotage the success of the whole team.

WHAT LEADERS NEED

I interact with leaders all around the world and have consistently heard the most successful claim that their greatest measure of personal and professional success has more to do with their interpersonal skills than their talents or trained skills. You and I can be exceptional at accomplishing our job description; but if we cannot get along with other people, we are bound to fail. Getting along with those in our fan club is beneficial. Helping "prickly people" along is even more influential.

What do we need?

We need to get better at *chasing porcupines*. We need to be intentional in leadership, instead of being impulsive. We need to be prepared for the moments when we experience *prickly people, prickly situations and our own prickly feelings!*

WHAT YOU CAN EXPECT

This book will simplify the principles of leading during difficult times, give you practical ideas for implementation, and provide inspiration for you to consider when leadership starts to feel uncomfortable.

You are about to be surprised!

CHASING PORCUPINES

Look up, it's a blue sky; interrupted occasionally as a gentle breeze persuades a small cluster of white clouds to move along. The forest is cool, trees swaying as they cast a comfortable shadow. Wildlife scampers through the underbrush. You are out for a much deserved morning hike following a well marked path at a brisk pace. The warm sun on your back and fresh air in your face creates the balance of a perfect morning. Suddenly you realize that you have walked unintentionally into the personal space of a porcupine. Your intrusion has startled both of you. The porcupine freezes momentarily as it tries to decide if you are a threat, then it begins to turn for a quick retreat. You, on the other hand, are in full stride and it takes you an extra step to halt your progress. All the while, your mind is racing through a safety plan and you realize two options exist: turn and run, or freeze and let the porcupine move on. But what if the porcupine feels threatened and chooses to assume the defensive position?

Most of us would choose to turn and run. A few people would stop like a statue and give the critter room to roam. And a small minority would decide to chase it!

"Chase it!? Wouldn't that be dangerous? After all, it can shoot those painful quills right at you and then you'll be sorry!"

Oh come on, where is your sense of adventure? You're out for a morning of discovery; a porcupine chase may just be the experience of a life time!

"Are you kidding? We've been taught to have nothing to do with porcupines. The best thing is to give them a wide berth and avoid them altogether! If you want to chase them, fine. Go ahead. I think you're nuts, but that's your problem. I'll play it safe, thanks."

Alright, I'll concede that you have a point. (No pun intended.) We have been taught to stay away from the prickly little critters. It has been said that when they are threatened those barbed quills can be shot at the approaching enemy. The best thing is to just let them alone.

However, leaving them alone because we might get hurt is reacting to a situation based on false information. Porcupines are not aggressive animals and they cannot shoot their quills. They do not have a projectile propulsion system built into their posterior! That is a myth. The quills are sharp, barbed and will easily dislodge on contact, becoming a painful problem for the aggressor. It is an effective defense system, but shouldn't be our reasons for avoiding them.

"Ok, I get your point! [Pun intended] Still, I don't think that chasing them is very intelligent. All I want is to mind my own business, take this walk

you're talking about and enjoy the journey without any unexpected confrontations."

I know. That is what I desire as well. Truth is; that is what we all want in life. We can appreciate moments of adventure and new discoveries. We can even be amused when others try things that we might not do ourselves. Still, getting through life without confrontations, nagging agitations and painful problems is our common aspiration. (Hmm, that helps me appreciate the basic desire of the porcupine.) We don't want to live in a reaction mode; we want a positive existence without the distress.

It would be absolutely perfect if you and I could start today as if it were a refreshing hike through a peaceful forest. Here is the plan: we want to mind our own business, enjoy the wonders all around, feel the balance of good effort behind us and new opportunities just ahead, and not run into any conflict! That would be fantastic! But that is not the reality of this path we're on. We will eventually encounter unexpected moments when we have to make some choices on how to handle the porcupines. Do we turn and run, freeze and let others decide what to do, or chase it?

Depending on the situations you encounter, choosing to turn and walk away may be an appropriate and wise decision. In other circumstances, slowing down and consulting or deferring to others could be what saves your life. On the other hand, chasing porcupines still seems to be a foolish, haphazard way to manage conflict.

Stick with me.

There will be numerous moments in your life that the journey will be abruptly interrupted by porcupines. Porcupines need leadership. And that is when you should be prepared with a chase strategy.

DIFFERENT PORCUPINES NEED DIFFERENT STRATEGIES

Have you ever felt that little rush of heat in your face or the muscles in the back of your neck tighten up when someone has agitated you? Have you felt the power of indignation rise up in your thoughts when another person said or did something that seemed insensitive? Did you take action, speak up or withdraw? The reality of that moment is that you encountered a porcupine, a prickly person. Their behavior triggered a natural response, just as if you had discovered a real porcupine in your path while hiking in the woods.

Not all prickly people or situations will call for the same strategy. Some of those people are just as surprised by the "encounter" as you are. Those are the ones who will make an effort to avoid the discomfort by moving quickly away. Another prickly person that you might encounter is the one who also did not anticipate the crossing of paths, but their reaction is to be cross and assume a defensive posture. They are usually trying to protect what they perceive as their beliefs or boundaries. One other prickly person you may discover is the one who is in permanent "prickly" mode. They are the ones who have their back up; quills prepared and are daring everyone in their path to push their limits.

Prickly people. How do you lead such a variety of people? What strategies work best for different situations? When should you lead and when should you leave? Learning the secrets of World Championship porcupine chasers will equip you with a refreshing and simple perspective on how to lead others more effectively.

PART ONE

THE ART OF CHASING PORCUPINES

It is truly amazing how a small town nestled in the heart of a quiet, mountainous valley can erupt into a bustling expression of world-famous activity. Typically, this is a town of hard working people, content to be out of the world view, living life quietly in pace with the seasons instead of the big city traffic. This is a place where little kids hunt for tadpoles in the spring and sled down "mountains" of snow in their front yards after the snow plows drive by. The most exciting activities that the whole town comes out for are Friday night high school sports, the county fair and rodeo, the kindergarten Christmas program and the annual World Championship Porcupine Races.

Yes, Council, Idaho hosts and orchestrates a one of a kind event so famous that people have come from around the world to witness porcupine racing. Pamplona, Spain has the running of the bulls. Monaco has the Grand Prix. France has the Tour de Franc. Indianapolis has the Indy 500. Race tracks throughout the United States have "wiener dog races." But only Council, Idaho has porcupine racing!

Every July 4th, the community's celebration of American Independence includes a parade (where the children ride their decorated bicycles), a greased pig catching contest, bar-b-que, fireworks and the porcupines.

For this annual event a group of devoted individuals carry out the tradition of converting the High School football field into a "stadium" of delicate proportions. A protective fence outlines the official course. In the early years, there was no fence. The crowds of people lined the field and served as the boundaries; until a rogue porcupine chose to head toward the sidelines instead of the finish line. In those moments, the crowds would scatter in hilarious panic to avoid an "encounter" of the close kind. Now an orange construction fence keeps the critters inbounds, while the people sit in the stands or crowd around the boundaries to get a better view.

Teams consisting of a porcupine and two people line up at one end of the course. Each team member has a specific responsibility. One person is in charge of the "containment" – a large trash can. The other team member is in charge of the "guidance system" – a broom. And the porcupine is responsible for running.

Just before the race begins, the porcupines are lined up at the start by placing them in the cool shadows of upside down trashcans. After the announcer has introduced the respective teams and their "running mates", the human partners take up the appropriate positions – one prepared to lift the can, thereby releasing the four-legged champion; the other poised with the broom, ready to encourage a successful outcome.

Here is the challenge, porcupines do not care to run; they like to hide in dark places. Therefore, when the starter signals that the race is on, the porcupines do one of two things: run back into their shelter or run for another hiding place. That is when the team has to work purposefully. The containment person runs behind the porcupine ready to cover the critter in case it decides to attempt evasive maneuvers. The guidance person runs beside the cute little prickly pacer with a broom, padding its backside to move forward or redirecting from left or right when it chooses to run for the crowd instead of the finish line.

The results are comical and exhilarating! When the porcupines are released, some refuse to move and turn back into the shadows of their shelter. Others run directly toward the sidelines looking for a way out and never consider the finish line as an option. A few, with a little encouragement, start to waddle in the right direction as the crowd cheers them on! And one or two just take off in the right direction, needing no guidance or help from their teammates. (Sometimes the team mates are left behind in amazement, holding their respective tools of engagement while the spectators laugh at their delayed gratification.)

The winners become World Champions and have bragging rights back in the forest. The struggler can only boast to future porcupine generations that they were contenders and saw it happen. The winners will climb trees and grin as they tell the story of how they made it happen. The ones who rushed back into the shelter of the trash cans will hide in cool, dark places and will never mention it again.

Now the humans have a different perspective. They'll be talking for years to come about how difficult it really is to move a prickly team member in a direction they do not want to go. Laughter at the memories will echo through the years. A few may pass on the exaggerated tales of how they got stuck with a slow poke. (Sorry, I couldn't pass up the obvious joke.) And, I guarantee, everyone will be ready to tell you how they would do it differently if given the chance.

Does all this sound familiar? Chasing porcupines is very much like leading prickly people. You know what I'm talking about. People who are difficult don't like change and would rather stay in the comfortable shadows of their shelter than to venture out into the wide open. And when we do attempt to lead them, they bristle and resist.

So we try to contain and guide them toward the desired goal. Sometimes we have to go into containment mode. Other times we need to offer guidance; gentle encouragement in the right direction.

The most important principle in leading prickly people is to always remember that ***our responsibility is not to force them, but to direct them***.

Leadership Lessons from the World Famous Porcupine Races

Anytime we are leading others through difficult decisions or change, we should keep in mind that successful porcupine chasers know the value of their tools, use them purposefully, and always keep the end result in focus. We can lead others to a successful outcome. No, I'm not suggesting that you rush out and start chasing others with a broom; but I am suggesting that you apply the principles that those tools represent.

What were the tools used for Championship results? A broom, trashcan, boundaries, a team, and cheering partners! Each one of those tools has a significant role in the process and outcome of the race. They also represent significant insights on how to lead prickly people. Learn the principles of the tools and you will be better equipped as a leader. Apply the principles and you will decrease the conflict, increase your influence and build an environment for championship results.

Let me encourage you right now to become intentional in your reading of this section. Use a pen and the margins, highlight the ideas that are meaningful to you, focus on the principles and look for ways to apply them in your interaction with prickly people.

The Broom of Champions - Guidance

The purpose of the broom is to provide guidance. When the porcupine veers away from the desired goal, the team member gently directs the focus back to the finish line.

The Principle of the Broom:

Every person has the right to receive direction and meaningful information that helps inform their decisions.

The most effective broom in leading others includes:

- Information
- Inspiration
- Instigation

All three of these elements create a perfect "guidance system" while navigating difficult circumstances. Each one, in and of itself, gives the leader a means by which to motivate the members on their team. You will discover that each one has a strategic purpose; and that people respond differently based on their perspective or needs.

1) **Information.** People need information. They need it in order to make decisions. They need it to inform their minds (and their hearts) with objective data that will shape their perspective. Information provides a starting point for reasonable dialogue; the lack of it starts the downward spiral of assumptions, rumor, misunderstanding and suspicion.

There is an expression that I picked up from John Maxwell that has guided my interaction with all those that I lead, *"People will be down on, what they are not up on."* This is true. When there is a lack of quality information, people will not extend their support and will begin to create misinformation. The imagined details will undoubtedly lead to doubts and uncooperative attitudes.

People *will not be for* anything that seems to be uncertain. It is simply human nature to want to have enough information before making a commitment. We carefully dip our toes into the water before diving into the deep end. We delicately check the thickness of the iced-over pond before putting our whole weight on the frozen surface. We try the shoes on at the store, before we make the purchase. We test drive the car before signing the contract. We date before we get married.

Getting the right information always comes before cooperation.

People *will be for* ideas, new responsibilities and opportunities if they have been given the respect that accompanies quality information. The more information that you and I can provide them, the more we create an environment of trust and that helps to develop certainty.

Just like the broom in the porcupine race, the purpose of quality information is to encourage movement in the right direction. We do not use the broom of information to force people. But occasionally, when they start to chase ideas that are not a part of the values or purpose of the mission, we remind them of the goal, expectations, timelines and commitments that require our best efforts. When they start to resist new directions, we offer them the opportunity to have a meaningful conversation about the significance of the changes and how the outcome will be beneficial. When they start to rush backwards to a more familiar way of doing things, we redirect their attention to the newer methods and help them ask the questions that brings them closer to acceptance.

2) **Inspiration.** Many leaders get so caught up in the process of "getting the job done" they forget that people need more than just a project, they want a purpose.

I'm particularly intrigued by a classic definition from the 1960 Merriam-Webster New Collegiate Dictionary. It defines inspiration as *"1) Act of breathing in...2) Act or state of being intellectually or emotionally inspired."* When used appropriately, inspiration should result in that very definition! It should be a breath of fresh air that provides a sense of relief or a purposeful supply of reality. It should also produce thoughtful and heartfelt action. When leaders use inspiration as a tool of guidance, the direction it provides helps others to determine if the course of action being suggested is worthy of their effort or support.

There is a profound difference between the menial and the meaningful. When an individual or group perceives the expectations that we have of them as mundane and uninspiring, they will do only what they have to in order to get by. When we introduce change without giving time and attention to its significance, there will be resistance. Helping others understand the meaning of their personal effort and involvement is how leaders can provide a fresh perspective in a stagnant environment. A leader provides inspiration by taking the time to have meaningful conversation with those they lead; and clarifying the definition of what is truly important.

Why do some people resist the direction that we provide? Three reasons: limited perspective, lack of appreciation, and lagging vision.

- **Limited Perspective**. They resist because we have failed to put things into the bigger picture. Often the struggle that followers express has more to do with not knowing the significance of their role in the context of the whole mission. How does their contribution tie into this bigger experience? In what way does their unique talent compliment the team? Leaders are usually big picture thinkers, observing the now and anticipating the next stage. Not everyone is like that; therefore we must give them opportunity to gain a newer view point.

- **Lack of Appreciation**. Many people go through their entire career (and in some cases their entire life) without a genuine expression of honest praise and thanks from their leader. The most effective way to inspire another person is to offer a genuine expression of appreciation for the effort they bring, the insight they have shared, the sacrifices they've made or even the honest resistance they have given because things weren't clear. Their value to your success is significant. Their questions cause you to communicate with greater intentionality. It is imperative then, to be generous and genuine with expressions of appreciation. Disingenuous thanks will be easily identified and does more damage than simply depriving people of good information.

- **Lagging Vision.** I learned early as a leader that people need to be reminded systematically of the vision that drives our efforts. I thought that having an annual event to celebrate past success and to communicate the vision for our future was more than enough. After all, I woke up every morning with a passion for what we were doing; they certainly must have the same drive. That wasn't enough. In fact, I personally lost my momentum when I didn't have a more frequent reminder of my purpose. When we get wrapped up in the *routine* we lose sight of the *reason*. If your team members are lagging behind, it could be that the vision is lagging. I believe that people need inspiration every 21 days. Be intentional with the inspirational. Talk about the benefits, celebrate the success stories, revisit what is most important and you will help your team move closer to the finish line!

3) **Instigation.** There will be occasions when the broom of guidance needs to come in the form of deliberate instigation.

We sometimes have to speak directly to the complacent about habits that are not compatible with the standards of expectation. Those in our organizations that have historically "coasted" just below expectations are a critical drain on the morale of the rest of the team. Allowing them to remain substandard will only perpetuate a mediocre environment. Instigating a conversation about the expectations and offering an honest observation of how a person can improve should provide some form of action in direct relation to the goal. They will move forward or shrink back. Either way, you now know what it's going to take to lead them.

Leaders can often inherit good people who are simply content. They are content with the circumstances, their status, and level of expectations. In order to bring them along to a new paradigm, we must help them understand that the current methods may be acceptable, but eventually changes will leave them far short of the ideal. We may have to instigate a conversation that leads them to identifying a probable pain or undesirable outcome. When people can look beyond their current comfort and perceive what they personally do not want to have happen, a creative tension begins to gain a momentum inwardly that leads to an acceptance of new ideas and commitments. This instigation of discomfort is not mean-spirited; quite the contrary, it generates from a kindness that genuinely wants to see others grow and succeed. So the leader has to bring in the broom of guidance and point out the obvious, the outcomes and the options!

Finally, we will have moments that we must instigate a new direction by confronting the person who is deliberately attempting to destroy the efforts of the whole group. Usually this happens when someone feels that they are losing control or credibility. They want things to be done their way or no way. Great leaders will communicate with these prickly people by using the best information and tapping into meaningful inspiration. If these do not redirect the argumentative controlling person, leaders have to take a stand for what is best. Instigation may take the form of autocratic leadership.

When a porcupine takes off in a direction that puts others at risk, the team members have a responsibility to stand in the way and protect the crowd. The same is true of leadership.

We all can grow so comfortable in our experience that we fail to see the need to move a different direction. Instigation is pointing out the pain or the eventual pain, and inviting those "prickly people" to consider new opportunities or expecting them to change a problematic behavior.

Guidance helps prevent the potential of people getting hurt from the barbs of poor attitudes and the quills of harsh words.

World Champion Porcupine Racers know that any attempt to force their team mate forward will be met with sharp resistance. The best way to move them forward is to quickly provide the right guidance whenever they veer off course. Leaders must also be prepared to use the broom to redirect their team members as needed.

> *The Broom of Champions provides guidance through the skillful use of information, inspiration and instigation.*

The Championship Trashcan - Containment

The purpose of the trashcan is to provide shelter. When the porcupine panics or runs the wrong direction the can is used to regroup and realign.

> **The Principle of the Trashcan:**
>
> **Every person has the right to the shelter of a place or the courtesy of some time for contemplation.**

The trashcan is a temporary place to retreat. It can be a shelter for the timid or your defense for the grumpy! The timid may simply need a moment to muster up some courage. The grumpy — well, you may need to protect yourself and keep them from raging instead of racing. Whatever the purpose of your trashcan, it is important to remember that it is temporary, not permanent.

All too often, leaders surrender to the demands of the uncooperative and lose the momentum of the vision or the pace of victory. It is natural and expected to have a measure of hesitation with some team members. However, leadership hesitation could result in corporate hibernation. Containment is intended to assist in moving forward, not retreating or resigning.

When you start to sense that you have some prickly people starting to resist a new direction, give them a place for contemplation – your office, a brainstorming session, or the HR department. (Oops, sorry HR, I didn't really mean that.) Also give them the courtesy of some time to consider the options or their reasons for resistance. If they cannot articulate what concerns them, encourage them to think about it and then follow up to discuss their thoughts.

The Trashcan could be utilized in the following ways:

1) *Test Run ideas before making a commitment.*

I learned long ago that when leading people through any kind of change, it is wise to give everyone a short period of time to "try it on for size" and test the results. The bigger the change, the more time people need to sample it. The test run should include well defined expectations, start and end times, clear measurements of success and plenty of permission to discuss what is working and what could be done differently. Once the test run is complete, offer everyone opportunity to identify how they intend to help achieve the goal and make the commitment.

2) *Walk in the Decision for 24 hours.*

Big decisions are hard to make. Have you ever taken the time to weigh out all the options, expose the potential negatives, highlight all the positives, make a choice and still feel uneasy deep in your gut? That happens to all of us. It might be buyer's remorse or self doubt, but we all know what it feels like.

Jim had a huge decision to make. It was a career change and a major move that would uproot his family. The decision was even more difficult because his teenage daughter was in her senior year in high school. The opportunity was amazing on all levels: financial, geographical, and occupational. He talked it over with the whole family; found that everyone was excited and open to the new experience. Rejecting the offer would be considered foolish by all his peers. And yet, there was something not adding up for him. What Jim did next, taught me a great lesson on decision making.

Jim said, "I am at a place where I need to test my decision. I'm going to announce to my trusted colleagues my *conditional* acceptance. I will *walk in the decision for 24 hours.* If in that period of time I have complete confidence and peace of mind, then I will move forward. On the other hand, if there is any hesitation or concern after 24 hours, I will decline."

He gave that announcement to his family and only a few friends. Twenty-four hours later, Jim was packing boxes and getting ready for the move. I asked him to help me understand his process. He told me that during his years as a leader he had seen others make similar decisions, only to go on and live with a great deal of doubt. He didn't want that for himself or his family. "Steven, I know that I'm good at processing all the details with my head – with logic. I also know that every human being makes decisions based, not only on the logical evidence, but from the heart – the intuition. I had to find a way to let my head and my heart balance things out. If I didn't have confidence (peace) after 24 hours, I'd always be wondering if I did the right thing."

Your containment of 24 hours to test the direction before making it permanent could be a great way to balance the emotions and the expectations.

3) *Take a Break, Regroup, Try again.*

I know that this seems so obvious, but leaders tend to get in a hurry and focused on the end result; and when we do, we miss the cues that the rest of the team is feeling overwhelmed or possibly not convinced. That is why we should build into the process of our leadership a strategic evaluation and open communication during the race. The information we receive will help us know if there is need for a short break to make adjustments. Even when we have the best information, things change along the way and we need to regroup for the good of everyone involved.

4) *Create an environment where it is safe to learn from mistakes.*

That wonderful *Principle of the Trashcan* helps us realize the value of containment. We all need a safe place to try new things and to contemplate how we might succeed in areas that are outside of our confidence or competence.

We can create that kind of environment for those we lead by allowing them to see us try new things, learn from our mistakes and discover what does and doesn't work. We reinforce that safe environment by encouraging risk taking on a regular basis. It becomes safe for others when we *invite* them to discuss insights learned as opposed to *telling* them what they should have done instead! Build a safe environment by remembering this motto: People would rather be invited than to be told.

> *The Championship Trashcan provides the individual with time to reason and the leader with a means to build confidence.*

Boundaries – The Championship Course

The purpose of the boundaries is to provide clarity in the midst of chaos. World Championship Porcupine teams know that those orange construction fence lines are there to keep the race in bounds and the crowd safe. They also know that using the fencing (the boundaries) gives them another tool for guidance and could result in a faster, winning result.

> *The Principle of the Boundaries:*
>
> *Every person has the right to know the limitations and to have full access to the possibilities within them.*

The people we lead need well defined boundaries. It gives a sense of purpose, protection, provision and potential.

1) **Purpose – A greater sense of focus in the midst of the chaos.** There will be chaos. Guaranteed. Opposing teams, past successes, personal expectations, and miscommunication. In the midst of the chaos, your ability to clearly state

the purpose and point out what your team will and will not do, greatly increases the odds of winning and helps your team avoid the bewilderment of indecision.

2) **Protection – Keeps us from chasing alternatives that do not support the goal; and keeps the spectators from influencing the outcome.** There are thousands of good things that we could focus upon; but not all of them are the best things. Most alternatives are simply things that *alter* our desired direction. We must be diligent about staying on course. And yes, there will be spectators that have the guts to shout their opinions but not the courage to get in the race.

3) **Provision – This is what we have to work with.** When people on your team know that they have permission to solve problems, budget to accomplish the mission, and the strengths of other team mates to tap into, there will be greater trust and cooperation.

4) **Potential** – When "escape" is not an option, we become more creative in exploring the direction of our success.

I was hired by an organization to lead a particular group through some dramatic changes. I started the job anticipating a great deal of resistance. Instead, most everyone was eager to try some new methods and cooperated. The changes proved to be very beneficial and there was very little complaining. I chalked it up to my great leadership skills.

I learned later that the gentleman who hired me had actually done me a great favor a few weeks before I arrived. He sat down with the entire team and told them, "We've tried many different options to turn this around. None have worked; mostly because you didn't want it to work. Now, you have only two options. Cooperate with Steven when he gets here or I'm going to close this department down."

No wonder everyone was so willing to try new things! Creativity rises when there is no escape.

Team – The Interdependency of Champions

The purpose of the team is to provide the greatest probability of winning. A porcupine needs the help of the others to start right, stay on course and stride to a victory.

> ### The Principle of the Team:
>
> *Everyone's individual talent combined with the interdependent effort of others will increase the potential of winning.*

Championship teams are the result of everyone doing their part at the right moment for the right reasons. The Team approach provides a rhythm that influences potential and eventual success. When the team members are balancing the purpose of containment and guidance; each contributing their part at the appropriate moment, the odds of success multiply.

All too often I find one person attempting to do everything that needs to be done. That person may be capable of doing all the tasks, but in the long run becomes exhausted, resentful and enables others to not carry their weight. Instead of multiplying their potential, they are only adding things to their "to-do list" and dividing their attention. I frequently remind the people who work with me that our success is not the result of one person doing 21 things, but as many people doing one thing each exceptionally well. When unique people give their devoted attention to the one thing they do best and combine it with the best effort of those around them, they move closer to the goal line and a collective celebration!

Now here is a special insight:

The World Championship Porcupine Racing team <u>includes the prickly partner</u>!

In our daily interaction with other people, we would rather exclude the prickly ones. I know. I do what I can to avoid them as well. However, when we learn to work with them and lead them effectively, we might just discover that they have a great deal to contribute and with the right amount of encouragement they help us become champions.

Cheering Partners – The Encouragement of Champions

The purpose of Cheering Partners is to provide an environment where getting into the race is acceptable, risk taking is encouraged, and every effort is appreciated. When the Porcupine races begin, every team has support.

> **The Principle of the Cheering Partners:**
>
> **Every person needs to know that their efforts are appreciated by others.**

The World Championship Porcupine Races would not be as exciting if there was no crowd. The encouragement and passion that others express in the midst of the race is part of the excitement! Those cheering fans have a way of keeping the teams engaged in the effort and focused on the desired outcome. Think about it: once in a while a porcupine decides it doesn't want to participate. So the team members reluctantly shift back into an "oh well" mindset. However, when they hear the chanting of their fans, they pick up their tools, pick up the pace and sometimes end up winning the race!

Imagine your favorite sports championship series without the fans. All you'd have is two teams in a scrimmage. Sure they play hard. They even play to win. But when there's a crowd supporting them, the effort is more diligent and the energy is dynamic. Every team and coach knows the power of the home field advantage. It has more to do with the cheering partners than the familiarity of the place.

When you begin to notice team effort starting to fade, bring to each member's attention the expressions of appreciation from those they serve. Share the "high-fives" of upper-management with the employees on the front line. When customers express pleasure for great service, give the whole team the kudos! Celebrate when major milestones are achieved in a project. Remind the whole team of how their contribution makes a difference.

You may not have cheering fans lined up along the fields of your endeavors; but, you can create a winning atmosphere.

WE NEED A WORTHY GOAL!

Respect is the key to a highly motivated championship team. Leaders who use the tools to manipulate others toward a goal will probably get stuck. In my opinion, they deserve to get stuck. Leaders who lead by principles will enjoy a greater level of success, because those they lead will have greater confidence. People react to and resent manipulation. They respond to respect. Motivation becomes a natural result when everyone on the team believes they are respected and valued. That leads to a respect of the end result. People move in the right direction when the goal is meaningful and worthy of their efforts.

Before we start the race of champions we must be able to identify the goal, determine its value and then respectfully articulate that to those we lead. Most leaders can say, "This is the goal line." Great leaders are able to say, "This is what makes the goal meaningful." How does that make a difference in motivation? People would rather give their best to what is meaningful, than to that which is perceived as menial. Do the people you lead respect the goal? Is it worthy of the effort you are expecting?

Which "End" Are You Focused On?

You will not reach the championship level if your attention is always on the "prickly end". Managers, supervisors, and company owners who become preoccupied with negative, uncooperative people or circumstances soon discover that they are running in last place. Yes, you must be aware of the downside of the backside in order to lead effectively. Butt, (pun intended) true champions keep their mind on the goal while being mindful of the drawbacks.

THE CHAMPIONSHIP PRINCIPLES

Principle of the Broom

Every person has the right to receive direction and meaningful information that helps inform their decisions.

Principle of the Trashcan

Everyone has the right to the shelter of a place or the courtesy of some time for contemplation.

Principle of the Boundaries

Everyone has the right to know the limitations and to have full access to the possibilities within them.

Principle of the Team

Everyone's individual talent combined with the interdependent effort of others will increase the potential of winning.

Principle of Cheering Partners

Everyone needs to know that their efforts are appreciated by others.

PART TWO

I would highly recommend to you a trip to Council, Idaho for the July 4th celebration. The World Championship Porcupine Races are truly a one-of-a-kind experience. You will be amazed at the sight of such a peculiar event. You'll be even more amazed that for a few minutes on a sunny afternoon the prickly pacing brings everyone together. The differences that are represented in personalities, cultural background, languages, age and even political views don't mater. Everyone has something in common – the laughter that transcends our differences and the freedom to stand side by side watching something positive take place in spite of the bristling contestants.

I think the greatest lesson we can learn from the porcupine races, is that we can still find common ground and eventually victory in the midst of all the things that make us uncomfortable.

Well, you may not get the chance to witness the porcupine racing; but there will be plenty of moments when you feel like the porcupines broke through the barriers and raced right into your life. For those occasions I give to you, Part Two. It is a mix of practical "broom & trashcan" methods, application and some inspiration for those times when you encounter prickly people, situations or your own prickly feelings.

PRICKLY PEOPLE

You already know it – not everyone is very pleasant to be around. As you attempt to be a great leader, you will walk right into the path of prickly people. Some are just startled for a moment, others are just habitually mad. How do we walk with those who are momentarily upset and intentionally lead those who are monumentally uptight? We could have a dialogue about negative people and why they're negative. We could even target a few techniques on how to manage them. That might be helpful. However, I'd like to suggest that we not get diverted from a more important approach for leadership – the importance of our own attitude and mindset when we do encounter the negative people. Consider this as Championship Broom training.

Remember that most prickly people will respond by retreating, resisting or racing. The way you approach them will make all the difference. So let's look at:

- Our personal attitude toward prickly people,
- What approach is best to move them along,
- Ways to communicate and motivate more effectively.

Developing Your Greatest Resource – "Relationships"

The most successful teachers, managers, politicians, and leaders who work with people know this simple fact: the relationships you develop in life will make or break you. It is true in your personal or professional life. Your greatest resources are the relationships that encompass you. The key to your personal growth and success has little to do with the technical skills, a plump financial portfolio, or the title of your position. The key to your success is how you develop those relationships with people.

I'm one of those people who enjoy words. I like to learn new words, meanings and if you give me enough time I'll dig deeper into their definitions and roots to see if there is something new to learn. So bear with me as I dissect "relationship" and the distinct attitudes that we bring to our understanding of that word. Which of these is your experience? Which would better help you succeed?

Attitude #1 - Relation SHIP.

Let's start by breaking the word down to its core.

RELATION: "A natural association between two or more..."

SHIP: "A large vessel built for deep water navigation…"

Say the word relationship and prior experience might cause some people to think of relationships as a big old battleship. We can laugh about that, but many of us treat others in that way. We think it is too difficult. "I'm in over my head and I can't stand it!" With this attitude relationships become an uncharted and frightening necessity that we must somehow navigate through. And the emphasis is on "through" because we don't plan to stay long.

Attitude #2 - Relation – ship.

A truer definition.

RELATION: "A natural association between two or more…

"SHIP: "Quality or condition…"

When you and I can develop relationships with this definition and attitude, we step incredibly closer to meaningful success. We understand that wherever we are there will be "natural associations" with others. Some will be significant, while others will be temporary. And yet, we develop our greatest resource when we focus the emphasis on "quality or condition". It is the commitment you make to quality in any relationship that makes or breaks you. Harvey

Firestone said, "You get the best out of others when you give the best of yourself."

How can you develop quality relationships?

Make an advance decision that all relationships deserve your best attitude. No matter where you are, in deep water or not, you can still choose your own attitude. Your actions then will influence the results. Choose to focus always on the quality; even when you know the relationship will be brief. Leave others glad in the experience of your moments together. This personal commitment will impact the attitudes of others and may change the way they see relationships. That would be a wonderful testament to your success.

The Practice of Love

Love is the greatest motivator. We tend to do what we love to do. We spend time with those that we genuinely love to be with. And those that we lead will gladly be a part of the team if they know that you and I care about them as individuals. Leadership by means of love and respect creates an environment of trust. Leadership by fear tactics creates apprehension and hesitation in the workplace. Jan Carlson, past-chairman and CEO of Scandinavian Airlines, suggest that there are two great motivators in life: fear and love. He said, "You can lead an organization by fear, but if you do, you will ensure that people won't perform up to their real capabilities." Love is a motivator that leads us to greater accomplishments.

Unfortunately, loving leadership is not common in the culture of today's business world. It really seems quite out of place. Love is not something we do very well. Yet, it remains the one thing we all need to succeed. What we need is to admit that in order for love to have its fullest impact – it will take practice.

Now before you dismiss this whole notion of love as a great leadership tool; let me clarify a general understanding – I am not suggesting a "warm, fuzzy, hold hands and skip down the hallway together" kind of love. We all have different definitions of love. People have thousands of interpretations of love. Some of us came from homes where love was expressed often with hugs and pats on the back. Others only heard the words "I love you." I came from a balance of those two worlds. My Father's family is Scandinavian and when love was expressed it came with a brief hug and few words. If it had been said once, that was enough. My parents were very generous with the words and our home was always filled with practical expressions of love. On the other hand, many people that you and I interact with on a daily basis do not have a positive memory of what love is like. And yet, everyone I know has a common definition of how it should be expressed. Love is genuine respect.

Effective leaders realize that respectful interaction will only be improved and strengthened with practice. They put into action simple commitments that help them to practice "loving leadership" on a daily basis.

Effective leaders...

- Model and practice the attitude of forgiveness.
- Do not ignore problems, but face them head on with respect that is tough and reasonable.
- Know that love is the essence of their character.

- Encourage the hurting and stick with them until they achieve their victory.
- Know that leading with love, not judgment, opens people's minds and hearts to new possibilities.

To have a lasting impact in your life, home and workplace you must put respect into practice. Model it, expect it from others; and in time you will discover that it is the wisest investment you have made. The returns are fantastic!

The Secret of Effective Communication

Home Improvement was one of America's top TV sitcoms in the 1990's. It was a powerful and extremely funny example of the need for better communication. The primary character, Tim Taylor, was consistently making a mess of his career, relationships, and meaningful conversations. Why? He had not learned the secret of effective communication. Tim was famous for taking the sage wisdom of his neighbor, Wilson, and twisting the "proverbial" advice to the point of hilarious confusion. In one episode, Tim and his business associate Al, are found ice fishing. Al wanted to talk. Tim wanted to watch "Gilligan's Island" on the portable television. They reached a compromise. Tim turns down the volume and says, "O.K., let's talk. You talk. I'll listen while I watch the show. Trust me, I can do this. I do it all the time when my wife wants to talk."

Tim needed to learn two simple elements that would have revolutionized his relationships. First, communication always involves sincere listening. Secondly, effective communication is always *relational* in its nature.

Effective communication is a vital ingredient to your personal success. Your business depends on it. Your most significant relationships will suffer without it. Closing that big sale, hinges on how effective you communicate. Putting into action the two simple elements mentioned above will increase your confidence and others will have greater confidence in you as well!

REVOLUTIONIZE YOUR COMMUNICATION EFFECTIVENESS WITH:

1. **Sincere Listening.** For communication to be successful two things must be accomplished: the message must be communicated and the message must be received. Most of our efforts to communicate break down because we are not listening. Oh, sure we might hear something; but we are often preoccupied with what we want to say next. Listening must be sincere. Set aside your own motivations and try listening to what is being said. You might hear more than just words; you might hear the

real meaning, needs and ideas. Ask yourself, "Am I receiving the real message?"

I learned this lesson the hard way. My youngest son came home from school and started talking to me about something that he had done that day. I was involved in my end-of-the-day ritual, TV news playing and the newspaper in my face. While he spoke, I responded with an occasional, "Hmm, that's interesting." Suddenly the television was muted; he politely took the paper from me, and placed his hands on my cheeks, looked into my eyes and said, "Dad, this is really important to me."

Aaaugh! I couldn't believe that I was giving him the impression that he wasn't important to me! That was the last thing I wanted him to think. And yet, he was absolutely right, I wasn't sincerely listening.

Are you?

2. A Relational Focus.

I'm going to show you the most exciting reality of communication. Look right into the middle of the word:

COMMUNICATION

What do you see? The secret is right there! In the middle of real communication you find a powerful focus – the letters **U – N - I**. The real success of authentic communication is to understand that there is always a "we" emphasis. The focus should always be "you and I". We are in this together! True understanding will be accomplished when I care about the other person more than the message and they care about me in the same way.

Leaders Learn To Listen

The great leaders that I have known are individuals who readily admit that the skill of listening is difficult. Primarily because there is so little time to do all that needs to be done. And yet, those same great leaders are the very people that model exceptional listening skills. They have chosen to be disciplined in the practice of listening, because they have found that what you hear reveals how you should lead. When you hear that someone has the wrong information, you lead them to the correct sources. When you hear that a person is excited about an opportunity you lead them to a point of empowerment. What you hear, gives you evidence in how you should lead. Listening is a discipline that can be learned.

My father tells the story of a unique day in his life. It took place on the Washington State shores of the Pacific Ocean. He was taking a quiet walk along the beach when he came upon an unusually large pile of drift wood. The sight of the twisted mountain was fascinating and he drew near for a closer look. While climbing through the rubble, he discovered that a large cave-like space was in the center of the driftwood. It appeared large enough for man to stand in. He pulled away a few of the limbs and weathered branches, then climbed into the cavity below. That's when he discovered a powerful lesson – a lesson he shared with me. When my father entered the shelter there was an immediate awareness that something was different. It was quiet. He poked his head back out into the daylight and the roar of the ocean, the whistling of the wind was there. But just inside there was no roar, no whistling – only the quiet. It was in the quiet that he learned the valuable lesson of listening to the really important things.

Your world is filled with the roaring of decisions and deadlines. Sometimes all you can hear is the whistling of things yet to be completed and people who need your attention.

"Oh! I can hardly hear myself think! And you expect me to learn something about listening to others?"

Yes. I believe that we can *learn* to listen. It doesn't come naturally for most of us, but we can learn the skills.

I'm going to share with you some basic points about listening that I found in my "Sunday Notes". Those are the notes I take when I hear a good message from a preacher that knows how to communicate. (Notice that I used the word message and not the word sermon. I don't listen well to sermons, because those are by definition: *a boring harangue*. A message, in contrast, engages me and inspires me to grow.) I wish I could give the preacher his due, but the notes are older and I can't find his name. I'll use his outline and give you some of my thoughts of how to put it into practice.

Five Keys to Skillful Listening

1. I need to REMOVE some of the obstacles.

The first step to discovering the important things in what is being communicated is to set aside a few of the items that are in the way. For example: unforgiving attitude, past experience, titles or position.

2. I need to RETREAT to a quiet shelter.

The distractions that keep us from hearing each other are numerous. Make the effort to move into a private and focused conversation. *Minimize the distractions to build positive actions.*

In his book, <u>Principle-Centered Leadership</u>, Stephen Covey suggests that we "consider the value of a private visit with each employee...a private chat with a client or customer – a time when your attention is focused upon that person, upon his or her interests, concerns, needs, hopes, fears, and doubts." Wow! Can you imagine the results?

3. **I need to REPEAT what I am hearing and understanding.**

We don't always hear the true meaning because it is clouded with uncertain words. Increase your understanding by taking a moment to verify what you *think* you heard. Repeat what you understand and ask if that's what was meant.

4. **I need to RESPECT the other person.**

Test yourself on this one. Who do you listen to more diligently the family member who has always encourages you or the guy at work who has the reputation of stretching the truth?

If I respect you, I will actively hear what you say. We may not always agree, but we do care enough to take the time to listen.

5. I need to RESPOND with empathetic action.

If you want something good to come from the effort of listening, then make the commitment to do what you can with what you hear. Change what you can, acknowledge the differences, and strive for a mutual success. Listen with a commitment to produce solutions.

The Power of Praise

The power of praise is the energy of success. Where there is no praise, there is no passion!

An incredible gift is offered when you give a genuine word of praise to another person. If you desire to fan into flame an atmosphere of joy in the workplace, give a little praise.

A manager has the ability to lift an individual up or to tear them down. When you identify an area of another person's work that must be improved or changed – by all means bring it to their attention. But if you want to energize their creativity and enlist support for the changes you must lead them through, find something in their work that deserves recognition and praise. Balance your *redirection* with *praise* and you will discover more motivated workers.

> *"Confidence withers under fault finding." - John C. Maxwell*

I have a confession to make. I am one of those fathers that comes unglued at the local little league baseball games. I shouted and pounded my feet in disgust every time the umpire made a bad call. I booed and hissed when the other teams got a hit. I moaned and groaned when my boys were tagged out. This baseball thing came close to causing me to have some health problems.

I have another confession to make. I *didn't* do any of those obnoxious things out loud or in view of other people. I kept it all inside! Truthfully, I am a fairly quiet, supportive dad. All I expected of my boys was the best that they could do. I knew that it was just a game, and they were simply learning. I also knew that if a child had a coach who didn't understand the positive value of building confidence – the kids were in for a long season.

John Maxwell says that "confidence withers under fault finding." I agree. I see it happen every day in the marketplace, in education, churches, and politics and even on the little league fields. For a quick view of this powerful truth take an afternoon and visit a few ball games. It won't take long to identify the coaches and parents who need to learn how to build confidence. Every time an error is committed or a child misses the ball, you'll hear the impatient voices focus on the mistakes. The more an individual hears about the mistakes they've made, the less confidence they have in their abilities. The more criticism is heard, the less desire an individual has to even try. Continued focus on what we do wrong, prevents us from learning how to do it right.

If you want to get the best from your team members (ball team, family or even at work) start to focus on their strengths and teach them in the areas of their challenges. The best coaches take the time to praise the individual for effort and seize the moments to teach where there can be improvement.

The impatient coach yells, "Don't do that!"

The great coach says, "Do it this way."

Which one do you think will earn the admiration and respect of the team? Which one will get the greater results?

Confidence withers under fault finding. Confidence grows in the presence of sincere praise and thoughtful teaching. Team-confidence or self-confidence is determined by your focus.

Three Practical Applications:

- Identify two things that you can do that will build the confidence of your family today.
- Make a list of three things your colleagues are doing well and let them know. List one thing you can help them do better.
- Stop fault-finding in yourself. Start focusing on your opportunities!

Lead with Praise

A team leader in my company came to me in a weary and discouraged posture. He spoke about a variety of concerns; some personal and some related to his team efforts and responsibilities. The stress of trying to make the right decision under the pressure of making the convenient choice had taken its toll on this guy. Normally, this man was full of energy and ideas; and yet during our meeting, I felt the heaviness of his heart. He believed that he had come to the end of his best efforts. He hit the wall of discouragement and was stunned!

He finished telling me his story. It was my turn and I had a choice. I could tell him the usual, "Well, I know how you feel. I've been there a few times myself. In fact, I remember a time when..." Or I could be his leader, lift him up and help him focus on the bigger picture.

Three feet from my chair sat Mr. Defeated. What could I say or do that would make a difference? Leaning forward in my chair, I made eye contact – we were face to face. (I do not visit with people from behind my desk. I remove that barrier by coming along side of them.) He took a deep breath. I spoke the most important words he could hear that day.

"I want you to know that I am proud of you."

I wish you could have seen his reaction. He almost fell out of the chair! He swallowed. His eyes opened wider. He was doing a mental instant replay to make sure he had heard correctly. My words were not what he had expected; but exactly what he needed. When this team leader left the office he bounded out with renewed confidence.

The power of praise has the ability to change attitude, performance and relationships. It is not what we have grown to expect from our leaders. However, it is exactly what we need from them; especially, when we are uncertain of the next steps we should take. When you praise another person for their efforts, when you let them know that you believe in them, you create an opportunity for a rediscovery of confidence and hope.

Looking for the good in others is more exciting than tripping over their faults. The power of *honest* praise has the ability to lift individuals and organizations from the ho-hum existence to amazing accomplishments.

Now take a close look at the following ideas for application and notice that this applies to every aspect of life. Where could you start leading the way with praise?

Three Practical Ideas for Application:

- Say to your kids: "I'm glad I'm your dad!" "I'm proud to be your mom!"
- Take 5 minutes to find a reason to praise a coworker or associate. Recognition is a highly valued form of creating job satisfaction.
- Send a thank you to an associate for a "job well done". Make it a genuine, old fashioned note; instead of an email. You'll be shocked by the results.

Spotlight the Positive

Who gets the most attention in your workplace or organization? Is it the team player who keeps giving her best to the game plan or the obnoxious spectator who offers nothing but criticism? Could it be the worker that quietly improves the day by performing better than average or is it the employee who moans and groans if asked to improve their performance to an average level? Could it be the individual that is glad to be a part of the organization or the one who complains they are stuck and deserve a better situation?

If you could choose one of these people to join you for lunch; which one would be your first choice? If you were marooned on an uninhabited island, who would you rather have as a castaway neighbor? My guess is that you would choose the more positive and pleasant individual. Very few of really enjoy being around whiners. In fact, most whiners I know wouldn't choose a whiner to be stranded with either. We like to be around winners; people who add value to life and are refreshing company! Team players that give their best are preferable to the takers who rob us of our joy.

But, who truly gets the most attention in your workplace? The "squeaky wheel" is usually the person who demands and undeservedly consumes our time and attention. The complainer bends our ear; then complains that we won't listen. The gossipmonger gripes behind closed doors and then talks about us behind our backs. The negative cycle continues to erode the positive environment we truly want to have; and still we provide a platform for the ones we would not take along on a pleasure cruise. Each time we entertain criticism, the negative person moves closer to center stage. It would be great if we could simply help them find the trap door.

You can change the negative influence in your environment by using the power of praise. Start the positive change by improving your performance in the following areas: attitude, words, and boundaries. When you begin to encourage the praiseworthy, instead of spotlighting the "understudy", the atmosphere of your organization will change for the better!

Put the spotlight on:

1) **Your Attitude.** Check first to see if your attitude is a contributing factor to the negative environment. Your positive attitude is contagious. Smile and others will smile.

2) **Your Words.** Give more praise to those who deserve it. The more you speak praise of another person, the greater their joy will be. The more positive your words, the less comfortable complainers will be in your presence.

3) **Your Boundaries.** Communicate your commitment to building others up; then prove it by avoiding conversation that discredits another. Yes, people will probably think you're a little snobbish; but they will be glad you practice the same courtesy when they are the subject.

It doesn't take long for "squeaky wheels" to stop whining when they discover you have no plans to grease them up.

The Bell and the Hammer

"Is it the bell that rings, is it the hammer that rings, or is it the meeting of the two that rings?"
- Japanese Poem

Hundreds of years ago a great bell was forged by the hands of the best craftsmen in the nation. When it was completed the men tested the bell for quality. The superintendent placed his thick hands on the surface of the bell and checked for any ripples in the metal. Satisfied, he reached under the bell and took a strong hold of the hammer. He gave it a swing. Suddenly a deep, beautiful tone resonated throughout the factory. The craftsmen stood in solemn respect and nodded their satisfaction. This masterpiece, commissioned by a prestigious town in the Mid-West, was ready for the long journey. The bell was carefully wrapped, the hammer secured and all was loaded upon the train.

During the journey an amazing thing took place. The bell, now awakened to its purpose, claimed sole responsibility for the ringing. The hammer also came to a similar conclusion. It thought that the beautiful ringing was a result of its strength. The townspeople would certainly be able to tell that the ornate bell was only decoration, and the tone of success was the gift of the hammer.

On arrival, the townspeople lifted the bell to a tower and waited for the magical moment.

The bell wanted to sing to the whole world. It strained to ring – with no result. The hammer could not let the bell steal the show, so it grunted in an effort to produce that unforgettable tone. All to no avail. Each had become so self-absorbed that the very idea of working together was repulsive. The bell whispered to the hammer, "Don't come near me." The hammer growled in response, "I don't need you!"

While the two achieved nothing, a kindly old man climbed along side of them and attached a rope in a strategic place. Upon returning to the ground, he pulled gently on the rope. The bell and hammer began to move closer to each other. Each tug of the rope brought them closer and closer until they met once again. The result was a long echoing ring and jubilant cheers from the crowded square below.

This is the lesson of team work. Reuben Welch once wrote: "We really do need each other." It is only when we come together that productivity and success can be realized. If we embrace the truth of this reality, the rewards are multiplied beyond measure. Shared responsibility brings strengthened relationships, trust, expanded networks and future success. However, when we ignore the principles of this lesson, we become ineffective and all progress is short term. Self-focused resourcefulness brings only minimized results, limited potential and weariness.

PRICKLY SITUATIONS

You already know it – not every situation is pleasant. Most of the negative situations that we run across are unexpected. Even more disconcerting is the fact that no one warned us it would happen and the wonderful world of higher education did not teach us how to deal with it! I remember the first board meeting that I had to lead. I walked home that night wondering what happened and why my college degree didn't prepare me for the "real world". You probably have some similar memories. Prickly situations cannot always be anticipated, but we can be better prepared for them.

Prickly situations reveal the need for intentional self-leadership as well as interpersonal leadership. Consider this as Championship Trashcan training.

You don't have to get stuck, others don't have to get defensive and the darkest moments could be the most rewarding. Let's look at:

- Ways to Contain & Redirect Negative Influence,
- How Leaders Can Model Integrity,
- What You Discover with the Right Perspective.

How to Navigate the Negative

There's a great story of a man who found himself in an embarrassing situation. He was waiting at a traffic light when his car stalled. The light turned green as he frantically made every effort to start the car. His unsuccessful attempts were greeted by a long series of honking horns from the drivers waiting behind him. The honking continued until he stepped out of his car and walked up to the first driver, and said, "I'm sorry. But, my car won't start. If you would go up and give it a try, I would be glad to stay back here and blow your horn for you."

Unfair criticism comes in many different forms. The stinging nature of the negative words and attitudes can leave us with a huge desire to "let them have it"! Some criticism can be productive. It can give us tremendous insight for improving our lives and skills. Most of us have discovered that little good comes from mishandling the criticism of negative people.

If you are in leadership, you will have someone that feels responsible to "blow their horn" at you. Here are some practical suggestions for navigating through two common forms of unfair criticism: unsigned letters and the individual who represents the anonymous group.

Unsigned or Anonymous Letters

<u>Do not read</u> unsigned or anonymous letters! These are not legitimate forms of constructive criticism or feedback. An unsigned letter serves only two purposes: 1) to vent personal anger; and 2) to dispense pain or vengeance on another person. The anonymous letter is a cowardly attempt to hurt the intended target.

I have a policy in my office that we adhere to and communicate when needed: *"All correspondence deserves a careful and thoughtful response. Unsigned correspondence cannot receive a response and therefore does not deserve a thought."*

You have the right and responsibility to control the messages your mind receives. If you intend to improve your skills, abilities and relationships – constructive concerns and advice are welcome. However, you cannot improve upon a relationship with someone who hides behind the paper. Anonymous letters do not build your character, they attack your character. Protect your integrity (and peace of mind) by choosing to cooperate with only those who have the integrity to enter into constructive dialogue.

The Sole Representative of the Anonymous Group

Have you ever had someone say, "I don't like what you're doing and there is a large group of people who feel the same way I do"? Before you enter into a negotiation of surrender, consider a few simple facts that fuel this technique of negative criticism.

- The "spokesperson" is possibly alone in their position. Referring to a group is only a power play. After all, there is *strength in numbers*.
- If there are others, they may have only nodded their "agreement of grievance" in polite response because they don't know how to handle uncomfortable conversations with disgruntled people.
- The "large group" may only be one or two others.

Try the following ideas for handling the criticism of unknown parties.

- Politely state that you welcome dialogue for improved relations and change; but you have a personal commitment to only communicate with identifiable individuals.
- Ask the sole representative to name the group members or to schedule another appointment when they can attend and speak for themselves.

- If the representative excuses the others on the basis of their discomfort of face to face meetings; offer to meet with a neutral observer or invite the "group" to put in writing their concerns and submit it with signatures.

If "group members" will not come forward or cannot be identified, you are not obligated to accommodate their opinions. Help yourself to see the bigger picture and help the spokesperson to focus on the issues as they see them. Both of you will probably discover that the "group" doesn't exist, and the solution is a simple conversation between responsible adults.

Gossip – Wrestling with a Pig

Nothing makes a long story short like the arrival of the person you happen to be talking about.

Colin Powell, in his book <u>My American Journey</u> quoted a public relations officer as saying, "...when you wrestle with a pig, the pig has fun and you just get dirty." That is true of gossip. No matter how you approach it, with the appearance of sincere concern or apparent malice, gossip always creates a big mess. It always hurts the person being spoken of and eventually hurts all those who participate.

You and I can control our involvement in useless gossip. Here are three practical ways to control gossip in the workplace:

1) **Refuse to participate.** Make it known that you will not betray another. Loyalty to others in this matter will win the trust of those you work with. Do not talk ***about*** people, talk ***for*** people! The moment someone begins to talk negatively of an individual, focusing not on the performance but on the person, that is gossip. Constructive criticism pertaining to a person's performance is sometimes necessary in work related discussion; but it should be discussed only with that person – not behind their back. Negative conversation about <u>their person</u> is never necessary and always unprofessional. Don't talk about people, talk for them in

supportive ways. Find the positive and build others up!

2) **Reconcile the problems.** Communicate directly with the person that is concerned. Talk about the problem or the performance. Find out what the real issues are. Get the facts, not the perceptions. Then try to bring solutions to the relationships and the issues.

3) **Report to the people.** I heard John Maxwell once say, "People will be down on, what they're not up on!" The longer you keep people in the dark the more dramatic their imagined conclusions. If you allow them to come to their own conclusions without the facts, you stimulate the possibilities of gossip in the workplace. <u>Communicate</u> the truth. Bring people up to the proper level of understanding and you will <u>eliminate</u> the potential of gossip. If you don't keep them up on the information that is important and relevant to them, they will be down on your silence. The conversations will begin to take a low road approach on morale and eventually take its toll on productivity.

Here are a few other nuggets of insight from Powell's experience: "Never believe the first thing you hear….Don't let your judgments run ahead of your facts. And, even with supposed facts in hand, question them if they don't add up.

Something deeper and wiser than bits of data informs our instincts."

"A gossip betrays a confidence; so avoid a man who talks too much." - Hebrew Proverb

Practical Integrity – Walk the Talk

Integrity in the workplace is a popular topic in seminars and coffee room discussions. We all agree that the need for it is a high priority. We pride ourselves in doing business with individuals considered to have a high degree of integrity and would not knowingly trust our money or time with people who show a severe lack of it. We certainly would not hire a person we could not trust, nor would we confide in them. However, the reality of the workplace erases the fine veneer of appearances and reveals that, like it or not, we have to work with some unscrupulous people. People who talk about integrity are plentiful; those who practice it are exceptional.

Consider this real to life scenario. The company you work for provides a service to the community. You have assisted a potential customer over the phone, established a good rapport and determined a future sales appointment. Prior to the scheduled appointment, another sales person from your company seizes an opportunity and takes the account from you. This is a frequent problem and has not been resolved through management or intervention. It is a problem that will obviously happen again.

While you are sitting in the office contemplating a course of action a unique opportunity walks through the door. A new customer arrives for a meeting with your unethical colleague, only to discover that the sales person has forgotten the appointment. As a professional, you assist the customer and provide her with the information needed to make a practical decision. And the now the critical moment, do you take the sale meant for your colleague or do you supply them with the details to get the final contract? How do you remain honorable without getting walked on?

Practical integrity is harder lived than spoken. But the rewards for honesty and honor are much greater than we could ever calculate. As Edgar Guest so eloquently stated, your actions – not your words, will have a greater and lasting influence on those around you.

> *"For I might misunderstand you and the high advice you give, but there's no misunderstanding how you act and how you live."* - Edgar Guest

The sales story you just read actually happened. (Sadly, it happens all too often.) The receptionist, who observed the honorable sales person, was so amazed by their right actions that she made a choice to always route incoming prospects to their office first because she knew that the customers would receive the best service.

The next month the sales person of genuine integrity experienced a dramatic increase in commissions. The loss of one sale to a cheat, led to greater sales from a cheering partner!

The Fable of Two Buckets

"When fire and water are at war, it is the fire that loses." - Spanish Proverb

I heard a minister give a tremendous illustration that has now become a strategic part of my managing and leadership arsenal. Let me share the story as I recall it.

"There is a man that walks through your town carrying two buckets. The buckets are filled with liquid. One bucket has gasoline. The other contains water. Each time there is a fire in your community the man runs to the scene. He quickly assesses the situation. He briefly contemplates the contents of each bucket. He chooses the appropriate liquid, picks up the bucket and pours the contents over the problem.

You can imagine what happens when he chooses the gasoline. There is an instantaneous explosion. The fire doubles in size. All the people involved get hurt.

But when the man chooses to pour the water, the fire is extinguished. The cool water exhausts the fury and steam quickly replaces the heat. All the people involved are relieved.

If you could choose how the gentleman would handle your problems, which bucket would you want him to pour out?"

Isn't that a great analogy? That minister's point was to cause us to consider that we carry two buckets. Imaginary, yes; but very real in how we behave when things get hot. One has the fuel of criticism. The other contains the water of peaceful actions. As we move about in our world we happen upon little fires. The fires are usually started by heated discussions, ignited by gossip or critical opinions. Upon arrival we quickly assess how to use our buckets. When we choose to participate in sizzling conversations, we empty fuel on the fire and everyone gets burned. But when we choose to use gracious words or peaceful suggestions, everyone can be spared from the potential devastation.

There is an amazing thing that should be noted about the buckets we carry. Those who consistently use the gasoline eventually run out of fuel and "burn out" their network of friends. But those who faithfully pour out the water never have an empty bucket! And soon, to their delight, there is an entire bucket brigade standing ready for action.

That is the power of a positive personal influence.

What to Look for When It Gets Really Dark

If you are currently facing some very dark moments, or frustrating circumstances and feel like there is just no way things could ever get better, I'd like to encourage you to put this book down for just a few moments, take a deep cleansing breath and open your mind to a simple insight in the next few pages. Go ahead, put it down and take a breath. I'll wait for you.

Now, take your time and read this:

"When it is dark enough, you can see the stars."

- Charles Beard

The memories of my childhood are filled with wonderful adventures and great friendships. A few of my most memorable adventures were simple "camp outs" in the backyard. We would roll out the old sleeping bags, stare at the stars and talk for hours. We never knew who actually fell asleep first; it just seemed that the stories blended right into the dreams.   Now that I'm grown, I can't remember any of the tall tales that were imagined on those warm summer nights. But I do recall the incredible expanse of the midnight sky and the awesome display of star power!

The last light out was always the porch light. Dad would step outside long enough to remind us that we did have neighbors and being quiet was to our advantage. "Goodnight." The light went off. The giggles began. The light would come on again. My father's deep voice could be heard from the window, "Do you want to come in now?" We'd pretend that we were asleep. And the light went off again.

It was in that awkward moment that everything in our known world became mysteriously dark; darker than we could have imagined.

"Are you scared?"

There'd be a long silence for dramatic effect, then:

"No!"

We'd lay there in the grass with our eyes focusing desperately for some glimmer of familiarity. The darkness never lasted too long. The stars would begin to multiply before our eyes. Often so much light would gather in the sky that in order to get any sleep we'd have to cover our heads with our pillows. The constellations were too numerous to count. Shooting stars made wishing more fun than the local well. And the darkness...didn't matter anymore.

Now, as an adult, I understand it was the darkness that allowed me to experience the wonder of the light. Without the darkness I would never have known that the stars are always there.

We will experience dark times in life. Disappointments, delayed expectations, and devastating circumstances. As certain as night comes after day, we will have difficult experiences that are hard to understand. The familiar light on the porch may go out and the darkest moments may follow. Those are not comfortable times. And yet, the stars begin to shine for those who choose to look for them.

Whatever tough times you face – don't look at the darkness, look for the stars!

WHEN YOU ARE FEELING PRICKLY

You already know this — sometimes the prickly person is you. You don't have to admit it if you don't want to; but I will — *"I am not always happy, positive or pleasant to be around."* There, I said it.

Positive Thinking can make a difference in the way you approach life. It does influence the way you interact with others. The practice of positive thinking even creates a climate in which great opportunities begin to come your way. And yet, troubles are always present and sometimes we don't see the possibilities because we gravitate first to the inconvenient, the irritating and the inconsiderate. We have moments when we become prickly. The good news is that our mindset is a choice. We can always confront our own negative thoughts and choose to find the good in people and circumstances.

So, what can you do to overcome those moments when you are feeling anything but positive? How can you develop a more consistent, positive mindset? Consider this as strategic training for using Championship Boundaries — taking full advantage of all the resources and appreciating the limitations.

Clearing the Air of Conflict

The Memoirs of Barbara Bush give an account of a trip to Mexico. President and Mrs. Bush were hosted by the Mexican President, Carlos Salinas and his family. The group participated in the typical political events: dinners, tours, and visits among the people. The conversation focused, at one point, on the issue of the terrible pollution in Mexico City. President Salinas made a comment that was very disturbing. The school children of Mexico City painted the sky gray, not blue; and without stars, which they had never seen, because of the pollution.

Conflict experienced in the workplace can easily become a pollutant to our perspective and performance. Its influence on our self-esteem often produces personal hurt. Now most of the time, workplace conflict is the result of simple misunderstandings or thoughtless behavior. It is rarely intentional and frequently impulsive. A word or an action is perceived as a personal affront and we become consumed with that simple issue. The "moment of offense" becomes a "monument of oppression" and the hurt grows, expanding into a "mountain of obsession". Harboring personal hurt does immeasurable damage to your peace of mind.

The fascinating reality is that the hurt hounding you has probably been forgotten by the other person involved. They're moving on with their lives and you are stalled-out by the personal pain. Now, don't misunderstand me, a hurt is a hurt! But, how you handle it determines the depth of your character. You can let the hurt pollute your thinking and contaminate your attitude, or you can climb above the hurts to experience a better view of yourself and those with whom you work. The hurts can be used to strengthen your character and to build your people skills.

Here are two ways we can deal with hurt in the workplace.

1) **BURY IT.** Our natural response is to hide our hurt and wish someone else would take care of it. We want others to be responsible for it. The problem is that we are so skilled at burying the issues, no one knows what it is or why we are so irritable.

2) **BENEFIT FROM IT.** How do we manage that?
    - Put It Into Perspective. Was it intentional or just thoughtless?
    - Privately Promote Understanding. Go to the person and without accusation or judgment, clear the air. State the facts, ask for clarification or see if there is anything you have done that might have been misunderstood.
    - Practice Forgiveness. Forgiveness is the fan which blows the smoke away, allowing you to see eye to eye.

There is an old Hebrew proverb that says, "A man's wisdom gives him patience; it is to his glory to overlook an offense."

Don't Blow Your Screen Door Off The Hinges

There are moments that even the best of leaders get to a point of complete exasperation. The prickly person has chosen to be argumentative or combative. The difficult situation has escalated to unimaginable proportions. Negativity is permeating throughout the whole organization and your best efforts to clear the air have been ineffective. Your personal agitation has become total frustration, and anger is not far behind. Anger not managed well will become an explosive complication. Successful leaders have a healthy understanding of anger and how to use it appropriately.

A determined man in Westminster, California devised a plan to eliminate a severe infestation of cockroaches in his apartment. Apparently the landlords had ignored his requests for help; and he decided to take matters into his own hands. It was reported that he activated twenty-five bug bombs, closed the door to his home and left the area. When the spray reached the pilot light of the gas stove, it ignited – blasting the screen door across the street, breaking the windows and set the furniture on fire!

"I really wanted to kill all of them," he said, "I thought if I used a lot more, it would last longer."

According to the label on the canister, just two would have solved his roach problem. The blast caused over $10,000 damage to his apartment building; and the cockroaches were seen dazed, but still walking around just a few days later.

My dad used to make this statement when he was feeling frustrated, "A fool gives full vent to his anger, but a wise man keeps himself under control."

Anger is a reality and surfaces in all arenas of life: home, neighborhood, work and often at the airport! It is an emotion that is difficult to understand. We have all personally struggled with anger inside and we have been burned by the anger of others around us. It has the potential of creating great destruction. It impacts the very core of relationships. But, the greatest tragedy is how anger seems to control us, not leaving any peace of mind. Anger creeps in at stressful moments, manipulating and twisting the circumstances into unfortunate attitudes, words and actions. It produces an imbalanced life, where "losing control" is typical because we feel out of control.

Prepare yourself for a paradigm shift!

Anger is a good thing!

Now, don't get upset. The reality is that anger can be a positive motivator. It is hard to believe, but it is true. Your anger can be a tool for accomplishment. You can get your anger to work for good, instead of working destructively. How? First, *Understand the Motivation* and secondly, *Act Responsibly*.

Understand What Motivates Anger.

There are two basic types of anger:

- Anger that is an "abiding" condition of the mind. It is an anger that feeds on an ongoing emotion or problem. This kind is long lasting.
- Anger that is an "agitated" condition of feelings. An outburst from inward indignation. This type quickly blazes up and subsides.

When you can identify the type of anger that you're dealing with, you can then focus on the appropriate steps to manage it. If your anger is *abiding*, you know that the solution is coming to terms with a specific problem that is unresolved. If it is an *agitation*, you know that it is a temporary feeling and not worth the mental energy to give it a place where it could become an *abiding* condition.

Act Responsibly.

Most people *react* to circumstances. However, if you will monitor the motivation of your anger, your ability to thoughtfully *respond* is greatly increased. Ask yourself, "Am I *offended* because I see this problem as a personal attack upon my character; or am I *moved* to a feeling of anger because I see an injustice?" If you face personal attack, don't dwell on it. Instead seek to discover what is motivating the other person's anger. If there is injustice, let the energy of that anger lead to positive action to make things better.

Don't blow the screen door off its hinges over little things. Control your actions and take calculated steps to bring about resolution and peace.

Making Room for Personal Fulfillment

There is a lonely road that winds through a thick forest. The evergreen trees crowd right up to the pavement pushing each other for the right of space and light. The only blue sky you can see is right above the road. Occasionally a cloud drifts into view; but the miles stretch into a canvas of dark green walls, a blue ceiling and a black carpet with yellow stripes. Then the clearing arrives.

It comes as a huge surprise because the miles of forest have a hypnotic affect. You become so accustomed to the surroundings that you don't expect anything different. But the clearing suddenly appears as you drop from the top of a gentle hill, and in a split second all your senses are alive – you are awake and aware of the change before you. The clearing is so unexpected and inviting that you welcome the opportunity to stop for a while. Thick, luscious grass pushes the forest away from the road, creating a harbor for weary travelers. There is more. A short walk from the road, close to the shadows of the evergreens – an old stone well beckons you to a cool refreshing adventure. The antiquated well has served thousands of guests for decades. A dusty, bucket rests on the ledge, waiting for another opportunity to bathe in the cold water below. You oblige.

Taking the bucket and rope in your hands you begin the descent of anticipation. Lower and deeper the tools drop from your sight until you feel the rope slack and hear the splash. Success! The bucket is full. (It is funny how success feels a little heavier.) Hand over hand you pull the rope with delight like a kid at the beach with a brand new kite. Bending over the stones you peer into the darkness and there you see a small piece of blue sky – the reflection of your world above. Overjoyed, you splash more excitement than water and the bucket arrives to your waiting hands.

The water is cold and tastes sweet. But something is wrong. There isn't enough. You'd like to splash more on your face; but when you look there is not enough. Why? A closer look into the bucket and you realize that there are rocks in the bottom. Big rocks. Big rocks take up space.

"A bucket will carry water in direct proportion to the degree of its emptiness when lowered into the well. If there are rocks in the bucket, it will only be able to carry as much water. Send an empty bucket down the shaft and the filling will be more complete." - Calvin Miller

The rocks rob us of the greatest dream of all – fulfillment! The rocks are subtle. You hardly notice their weight until they begin to crowd out your joy. The most common rocks found in our buckets are *jealousy, pride and anger*. These are the ones that create the greatest trouble in the workplace. They are also the most destructive in the quiet depths of our "personal well". If you would like greater personal fulfillment check to see if there are any rocks crowding out your potential.

Personal fulfillment is the underlying hope in every written goal, unspoken wish and list of things to do. It is the heartbeat of every friendship and the dream of each new venture. Some people spend their lives searching for personal fulfillment, yet never find that peace of mind or contentment. I believe the reason for their disappointment is because they haven't made room for their heart's desire. Those elements of jealousy, pride and anger just take up too much space.

My three sons and I went fishing in an Idaho mountain river during our summer vacation. Have you ever attempted a fishing trip with three grade school boys? It is an unforgettable adventure. I started the "expedition of a lifetime" by equipping each boy – one at a time – with a pole, proper bait and their own section of the river. I should have prepared all three poles, and then started them out at the same time. As it turned out, when I began preparing the third pole, the first two boys were in need of my attention. One had strategically snagged his line on a rock and the other was exuberantly landing a large rainbow trout!

"Oh boy," I said to myself, "I'm in big trouble."

Our peaceful day at the river aggressively turned against me and "conflict" jumped to the occasion! I had to decide in a fraction of a second who to help first. Should I finish setting up the waiting fisherman, help bring in the "catch of the day" or run to free the rock bound line? (I am not good at multiple choice tests.) I jumped to my feet. We caught the fish, freed the line and finally baited the waiting hook. When it was all said and done, I looked up to see my three wonderful boys elbowing each other in an attempt to claim the "best spot" for catching fish.

I don't want you to get the wrong impression. We had a fabulous time. Everybody caught some fish and we really did enjoy being together. But, in those first few minutes we saw the most common enemies of joy invade our space and attempt to tangle the lines of our relationships.

Jealousy stood right next to my son who was waiting for his chance to start fishing.

Anger jumped on the back of my son who had caught nothing but a rock!

Pride filled up the breast pockets of my boy who had just out-fished his brother and caught his very first fish.

After I untangled the attitudes and put things back into proper perspective, we all had a "whopper" of a time! The boys learned to bait each other's hook and work together – sharing the experience.

Consider for a moment this important question. Are the lines of important relationships getting snagged by the rocks in your life?

Four Practical Applications:

- Evaluate your level of emptiness. Remove the rocks that prevent your potential!
- Give each other a little space to manage the emotions.
- Place a priority on being proud of each other's accomplishments and efforts.
- Be willing to help others when they are in trouble.

TOOLS TO HELP ACHIEVE YOUR PERSONAL FULFILLMENT

A tragedy was announced on the evening news. It was 1997 and the report of a plane crash captured the headlines. Guam. A 747. The plane smashed into the hills just above the airport runway. There were survivors. There were multiple deaths. I don't enjoy viewing the aftermath of tragic events, but on this occasion I couldn't help noticing that the wreckage was just a few yards from equipment designed to help guide planes to a safe landing.

The airport's glide slope equipment was out of service for regular maintenance. Further reports revealed that another tool for pilot navigation was not operating properly - the Radar Minimum Safe Altitude Warning System. The Orange County Register reported that "a properly working system could have allowed the pilot to be notified in time to pull the jet to a higher altitude." Two strategic tools that could have prevented the crash were not functioning effectively.

There are two strategic tools in your life that will help guide you as you make room for personal fulfillment. If functioning properly, these tools will prevent you from coming short of your hopes and dreams.

1) **Honesty**.   The evidence of sincerity, integrity and truthfulness.

There are thousands of people who *talk the talk*; the one who *walks the walk* is the one people trust. Hiding the truth and withholding information eventually reveals the altitude of your character. Living one way in public and another way just out of view creates double vision and a double minded person. People don't trust a liar or someone who is *fuzzy* on the issues.

Honesty in all circumstances makes room for personal fulfillment. You can live with a sense of inner peace and public integrity when you make *trustworthiness* a priority in your lifestyle.

"Never chase a lie. Let it alone, and it will run itself to death." - Lyman Beecher

2) **Humility**. The evidence of a teachable attitude.

Just as the airport equipment in Guam could have prevented a crash by signaling the pilots to make corrections in mid course, humility is the proof that one can make corrections in route to personal fulfillment. A genuine humble attitude shows that a person is open to change and instruction. It reveals that the person wants to grow in character development. In contrast, the one who is too good for instruction and boasts of having it all figured out is in danger of low altitude living. The result could be alienation and mistrust.

Humility is the companion of honesty. Together they provide the conditions for a successful approach to life.

Paying close attention to these indicators in your thought process will influence your altitude in life. When you need to bring things in for a safe landing, you'll know where you are in relation to the goal. When you need to "rise above" the mountains of negativity you will know the right altitude and be able to choose the right actions at the right moments.

The Magnitude of Your Attitude

Everyone knows that your attitude can determine the course of the day. If the supervisor gets up on the wrong side of the bed (or even the wrong side of the house) you can be certain that the day will be unpleasant for the employees. On the other hand, if the same supervisor is humming the Louis Armstrong classis "It's A Wonderful World" everyone will be more relaxed and optimistic. Attitude has influence!

Your attitude today can influence your posture. If you are downhearted, your head and shoulders will sag. If you are glad, your step will be quicker and may even have a hint of a skip or two. Your attitude can even influence your ability to think creatively. If you are discouraged, you will have trouble remembering your priorities for the day; but if you are full of hope, the solutions and ideas begin to flow freely. Attitude has influence!

Have you ever been around a person who habitually found something to complain about? How long did it take for you to get tired of their presence? How quickly did the exposure to a negative person cause you to be critical? It doesn't take long. Conversely, how do you feel when you have to spend the afternoon with a person of positive outlook and encouraging words? When it comes time to leave you wonder why the afternoon went so fast! Instead of feeling drained emotionally, you have a sense of being replenished. Attitude has influence!

There is an important word that can help us begin to develop greater and lasting attitudes. The word is **magnitude**. We don't hear it often in everyday language. It is not a word that frequents our dinner table discussions. The only time it seems to creep into our conversations is when it is used in reference to earthquakes. And yet, it has tremendous potential when combined with the right attitude.

Look at the definition of *magnitude: 1) greatness in size, 2) greatness in significance or influence.*

I love that second definition. *Greatness in significance or influence.* Your attitude has influence. The *"Magnitude of Your Attitude"* is the pivot point upon which you succeed each and every day. When we evaluate the great significance our attitude has on our family, clients, associates and prospects, we begin to behave in a more productive manner. The moment we realize the great influence our attitude has on the outcome of our tasks we gladly strive for higher standards.

Pause for a moment and consider this question. To what degree or direction are you allowing your attitude to go?

Here is the great news!

Your attitude does not choose you – you choose your attitude! And when you choose your attitude, you have chosen your direction.

How to Choose Your Attitude

I am not naturally a person who looks for the positive in all situations. My tendency is to scan for problems, mistakes or areas that should improve. Yet, many people perceive that I have an inborn ability to find the good in every circumstance. For instance, a long time friend was troubled by some uncomfortable personal issues and expressed her sincere apprehension. I could definitely see the validity to her concerns, but commented that there were also a few positive possibilities that could result. She looked at me and said, "Steven, you are always looking for the good in situations."

Really? How did that happen? It happened as a result of the decision to make it a habit in my life.

You can *intentionally decide* to be positive in life or *impulsively react* to life.

How do you choose your attitudes? One of two ways:

1) **You let the issues determine your attitude.**

"I think I'll wait for something to happen and then I'll react to the circumstances." In this manner we are always reactive and on the defense.

2) **You make the decision in advance.**

"What my mind is focused on is what I am drawn to believe or behave." In this manner we are proactive and have the power to be prepared.

I heard about a little boy who was standing in his front yard playing ball. He had a bat and ball in his hands. He'd take up a hitter's position, look at the ball with determination and declare, "I am the greatest hitter in the world!" Then he tossed the ball into the air, swung the bat and missed. "Strike one!" He picked up the ball, proclaimed "I'm the greatest hitter in the world" and threw the ball up into the air again. The ball descended. He swung and missed again. "Strike two!" The little boy examined the ball carefully and tested the weight of both the bat and ball. Then with more resolve he repeated the process one more time. He missed the ball and shouted, "Strike three! Wow, I am the greatest pitcher in the world!"

Becoming a person who believes and acts by the positive magnitude of attitude is the result of advance decisions and deliberate habits. It is not a natural inclination for most people. The positive influence of a great attitude is the conditioning of the mind and heart through the daily habit of looking for something good.

Here are some quick suggestions to begin developing the habits of a positive Magnitude Attitude.

Write down one good thing about your day. Do this every evening for two weeks.

Identify one positive thing about the person who causes you the most stress.

Nurture your new attitude with positive thoughts and values. Listen to uplifting music or read something that makes you smile.

Why "Positive Mental Thinking" Nonsense Doesn't Really Work

You can't sleep. It is late at night. The TV seems like a possible sedative. You flip through a variety of infomercials: The Magic Mop, The Dynamic Dicer, and The Jewelry Juicer (fresh nutrients and if you're lucky gem stones worth thousands). But wait there's more! You stumble on a new self help series that promises to reveal the secret to all success. Before you know it, you have ordered *How to Become a Mega-Power,*

Super Negotiating, Fire Walking, Ultimate Self! You soak up all the information you can from the CD's and bonus DVD. You read the book and begin with the first step in this *"...dynamic journey, with never before revealed secrets, guaranteed to improve your life or your money back!"* Wow!

What is the first step? Step #1 – Begin to tell yourself, with a tone of confident belief, what it is that you want in life.

That seems harmless enough, so you begin repeating on a daily basis self-affirming statements of belief. Such as: "I am a millionaire. I drive a Jaguar. I live in a 10 bedroom mansion overlooking the beaches of La Jolla, California. I vacation in exotic places. I am a millionaire!"

Day after day you repeat this statement. You know, because the book guarantees, that soon you will be wealthy. But after 21 days all you have is a habit of saying "I am a millionaire" and nothing has changed.

So you try another statement of *belief*. "I am happily married." This may be difficult to say if you're single or miserable in a marriage that has lost its spark. But, you keep saying the magic phrase day after day until you realize that nothing has changed.

What is wrong? Chapter 2 of this super book says it is all in your attitude! You have to believe and have a great attitude to back it up. Bad attitude equals bad results. Super, ultimate attitude brings mega results! Really? You are still dirt poor and struggling with your marriage. You must have missed something, so you get all hyped up again by listening to the CD's and DVD and 21 days later – nothing has changed. Except, your spouse is mad because the credit card bill arrived and there is this huge debt for something called *How to Become a Mega-Power, Super Negotiating, Fire Walking, Ultimate Self!*

Attitude built on hype or emotional psychology is only as good as the thrill of a world class roller coaster. It doesn't last. It feels good for a short time, but always returns to the same place you started from. Attitude based on wishes or even lies will prove to be a major disappointment.

However, if you support your wishes and dreams with an attitude built on truth, the results will be amazing! This is where I have to ask you to stop reading so fast and pay close attention; because this is not a secret, but a vital principle if you want to see real results.

Here is the key to the Magnitude of your Attitude:

Applying the truth is tremendously uplifting, deliberately effective.

That's it. It is not complicated, mysterious or only effective for those "special" people in the world who are drawn to its power. It is simple and makes all the difference if you are willing to honestly act upon it.

Now just in case you didn't notice how simple it really is, let me spell it out in another way.

Applying

The

Truth

Is

Tremendously

Uplifting,

Deliberately

Effective

When we support our dreams and hopes with an attitude built on truth the results are evident, effective and measurable. Even when the truth is hard to swallow it has a way of bringing us to a point of action. ***Desired Truth*** is easy to reach for.

Hard Truth clears the way for honesty and change. Truth always creates opportunity to grow in character. It also helps us identify what must be changed, eliminated, or started in order to achieve our desires.

> *The truth is always an action point! Find the hard truth in relation to your dream and take action now.*

Consider the millionaire idea again. Simply wishing to be a millionaire does not create a millionaire. But, if you acknowledge the truth in the dream, you will see that in order to become wealthy you must control spending and start saving or investing responsibly. Your attitude focuses on the truth of your circumstances and the truth is always an action point!

Remember, sometimes the truth is hard to accept, because it might reveal that we are partly (or totally) to blame. But if you want to improve, looking for the truth and accepting it is a necessity.

You want to be happily married. However, under the circumstances that dream seems to be crumbling under the tension and silence. What is the truth? At the moment you are not happy. Why? You are not happy because you never talk to each other anymore. You don't take walks on the beach as you did before. Maybe you failed to forgive each other for past issues. *Applying the truth to your attitude creates possibilities.* Possibilities are easier to work with than high hopes or wishes. You can do something!

Focusing your attitude on the truth of your situation always gives you the opportunity to take action. You can start doing something to improve or you can stop doing those things that are destructive. When you take deliberate action, you grow. The Magnitude of your Attitude will have greater potential when combined with a commitment to take the right actions.

Looking for Greener Grass

Finally, let us face the truth that there are occasions that we become prickly, simply because we have grown weary of trying to lead prickly people and work through negative situations. We'd like for the naysayers and whiners to either agree or leave. We hope that the difficult circumstances would just work out! They don't. So we begin to entertain the idea of making a change, going somewhere else, finding more pleasant people and opportunities.

Have you discovered that everywhere you turn, there seems to be another porcupine to lead?

Changing locations does not guarantee that you will be prickly free! Instead, it often reveals that sticking with a plan to lead would have been more beneficial; and choosing a different path only puts you back at the beginning of the race.

I once had an office building that bordered a dairy pasture. My window looked out upon the grassy fields. A panorama of the Cascade Mountains in Central Oregon could be seen practically year round. It was a peaceful setting that sure beat the view of city freeways packed with impatient and late employees. I have to confess that my surroundings really spoiled me. I couldn't imagine a better place to be creative. Nothing could destroy this perfect setting. Until…

I don't know how it started, but one day a curious cow had made her way to my office window. I must have been quite entertaining for she was watching my every move. Right there in my window was a white & brown, big eared, bug eyed cow! That irritated me. This was an invasion of privacy. She was blocking my view. Something had to be done.

I stepped over to the window and made an aggressive motion at the cow. I thought that might scare her away. She laughed. (Well, it sounded like a moo to everyone else; but to me, that foolish cow was laughing.) I went outside to the fence and waved my arms, shouting, "Get out of here! Shoo!

Scram! Yee-haa!" She looked at me with *udder* contempt, and then stuck her head through the fence to feast on my grass. This was insulting – so I marched back into the office and closed the curtains.

Months dragged by and that cow would come by every day and bellow outside my window. I did my best to ignore the taunting. However, on occasion I would open the window and make some comment about having steak for dinner. And that cow would stick her head through the fence and eat some more of my grass!

There are times that the peaceful setting surrounding our life or career is interrupted by obnoxious, uninvited circumstances; i.e. annoying people, pushy boss, unappreciated efforts, etc. We do our best to ignore the problem; but can't stop from the occasional flip comment or frantic waving of arms. We holler at people who think our reaction is funny and they care only about enjoying our green grass.

If we are not careful, we too may begin to look for a new patch of grass to call our own. We start looking for greener pastures in other fields; and what once was perfect, is suddenly less than adequate. But, let me remind you of the book Erma Bombeck wrote: <u>The Grass Grows Greener Over The Septic Tank</u>. Don't rush too quickly into a change because of irritations. Keep in mind that what bothers you right now, may very well be temporary. Rushing on to something different might actually be worse and that can really stink.

The best thing that we could possibly do for ourselves is to grow through the uncomfortable experiences. The new insights we gain will create leadership depth, credibility and greater confidence. It will also build the confidence of those we lead.

CONCLUSION

The Champion Porcupine Racers that stand on the podium at the end of the race are usually people who did not expect to win. Oh, they certainly hoped to win; but the variables that could have influenced the outcome must have tempered their hope with some hesitation. Think about it - you could get stuck, have an uncooperative partner, or be competing against a faster team. The risks are real. So are the porcupines! And yet, that doesn't stop people from stepping into the arena of competition. The fact that they got into the race in the first place makes them champions! It sets them apart from the spectators. Participating moves them closer to the winners circle.

The same is true for you.

There are risks involved in leadership. Anytime you attempt to encourage people to move in a new or unfamiliar direction, there will be some who get defensive and prickly. Don't let that discourage you from stepping into the arena. Be courageous, participate in the adventure, and move forward with confidence now that you know how to *chase porcupines with championship potential*!

ABOUT THE AUTHOR

Steven Iwersen is an internationally known keynote speaker, author, and noted leadership specialist. He is the founder of Aurora Pointe, LLC, a company devoted to the mission of developing leaders that lead from the heart and inspire excellence in others.

Steven has trained thousands of leaders from New York City to San Diego, Miami to Montana. His audiences have included leaders from Jet Propulsion Labs, US Air Force, New York/New Jersey Port Authority, FBI, Hallmark, Social Security Administration, and more.

Steven is a member of the National Speakers Association and has served as the president of the NSA-Heartland Chapter. He is known as a Keynote Speaker that breaks through the usual with the unexpected, inspires and involves the audience, and creates breakthrough insights.

For more information on having Steven speak at your event or to subscribe for free to his blog Leaders Viewpointe, visit **www.steveniwersen.com** or call directly 913-406-3824.

NOW WHAT?

Now that you have read the book *Chasing Porcupines: How to Lead Prickly People*, what are you going to do to become a leader that inspires others and creates a championship environment?

Take the next step and begin to enhance your own winner's mindset!

Visit www.chasingporcupines.com and take advantage of the FREE training lesson, ***"What Every Successful Leader Knows"***

You will learn the principles that will help you establish the habits that can dramatically change your life.

What Every Successful Leader Knows is available to you in audio format online.

VISIT US AT WWW.CHASINGPORCUPINES.COM TO RECEIVE YOUR FREE TRAINING LESSON, AS WELL AS INFORMATION ON OTHER VALUABLE RESOURCES

BRING STEVEN IWERSEN
TO YOUR ORGANIZATION

Steven Iwersen is an award-winning speaker known for his engaging presentation style.

He is a Keynote Speaker that breaks through the usual with the unexpected, inspires and involves your audience, and creates breakthrough insights.

There are hundreds of ways to communicate with your audience, boring them with the truth should not be one of them. Having Steven speak will help you create an experience and not just an event.

Don't hesitate a moment – bring Steven Iwersen to your company or convention for training and motivation.

For personal growth, call for customized coaching.

**TO BRING STEVEN IWERSEN TO YOUR NEXT EVENT,
VISIT WWW.STEVENIWERSEN.COM
OR CALL 913-406-3824**